Women of the Union

by Alice K. Flanagan

Content Adviser: Brett Barker, Ph.D.
Assistant Professor, Department of History,
University of Wisconsin–Marathon County

Reading Adviser: Rosemary G. Palmer, Ph.D.,
Department of Literacy, College of Education
Boise State University

COMPASS POINT BOOKS
MINNEAPOLIS, MINNESOTA

Compass Point Books
3109 West 50th Street, #115
Minneapolis, MN 55410

Visit Compass Point Books on the Internet at *www.compasspointbooks.com*
or e-mail your request to *custserv@compasspointbooks.com*

On the cover: Color engraving of a Union Army hospital during the American Civil War

Photographs ©: The Granger Collection, New York, cover, 5, 6, 7, 8, 9, 10, 12, 15, 23, 25, 26, 28, 29; Prints Old and Rare, back cover (far left); Library of Congress, back cover, 13, 14, 28, 30, 37; Mary Evans Picture Library, 16; Bettman/Corbis, 17, 32; MPI/Getty Images, 19; Museum of the City of New York/Getty Images, 20; Corbis, 21, 22, 24, 41; Charles J. and Isaac G. Tyson/National Park Service/ National Archives/Time Life Pictures/Getty Images, 31; Boston Public Library, 34; State Archives of Michigan, 35; National Portrait Gallery/Smithsonian Institution/Art Resource, N.Y., 37; College of William and Mary/Swem Library/Special Collections, 38; Courtesy HQ AIA/Art by retired Air Force Major Lori Alaniva, 39.

Editor: Sue Vander Hook
Page Production: Noumenon Creative
Photo Researcher: Abbey Fitzgerald
Cartographer: XNR Productions, Inc.
Library Consultant: Kathleen Baxter

Creative Director: Keith Griffin
Editorial Director: Carol Jones
Managing Editor: Catherine Neitge

Library of Congress Cataloging-in-Publication Data
Flanagan, Alice K.
  Women of the Union/ by Alice K. Flanagan
      p. cm.—(We the people)
  Includes bibliographical references and index.
  ISBN-13: 978-0-7565-2035-9 (hardcover)
  ISBN-10: 0-7565-2035-5 (hardcover)
  ISBN-13: 978-0-7565-2047-2 (paperback)
  ISBN-10: 0-7565-2047-9 (paperback)
  1. United States—History—Civil War, 1861–1865—Women—Juvenile literature. 2. United States—History—Civil War, 1861–1865—Participation, Female—Juvenile literature. 3. Women—United States—Biography—Juvenile literature. 4. United States—History—Civil War, 1861–1865—Biography—Juvenile literature. 5. United States—History—Civil War, 1861–1865—Social aspects—Juvenile literature. I. Title. II. We the people (Series) (Compass Point Books)
  E628.F57 2006
  973.7082—dc22   2006003943

TABLE OF CONTENTS

"Little Nurse of Gettysburg" 4

Women and the War 7

Support on the Home Front 12

Angels of Mercy 16

Famous Women Doctors 20

Courageous Nurses 23

Daughters of the Regiment
   and Vivandières 30

Soldiers in Disguise 33

Famous Union Spies 37

Glossary 42

Did You Know? 43

Important Dates 44

Important People 45

Want to Know More? 46

Index 48

"LITTLE NURSE OF GETTYSBURG"

Distant gunfire startled the people in the quiet town of Gettysburg, Pennsylvania. It was the morning of July 1, 1863. About a mile away, two armies were locked in battle—Southern Confederate troops and Northern Union forces. Fierce fighting continued for three days at the Battle of Gettysburg, the deadliest battle of the American Civil War.

In the center of town, 9-year-old Sadie Bushman was finishing her chores. Her mother yelled, "They are going to shell the town!" On her mother's orders, Sadie grabbed her little brother and fled to their grandparents' farmhouse 2 miles (3.2 kilometers) away. The house had become a makeshift hospital. Injured Union soldiers were everywhere.

A doctor asked Sadie to help. Although frightened by so much suffering, she began caring for wounded soldiers. Because she was so small, she had to climb onto the soldiers' beds to change their bandages and help them eat.

The doctors and soldiers she helped never forgot Sadie. Years later, the doctor who asked for her help gave her a house on his estate in San Francisco, California. She

The Battle of Gettysburg was considered the turning point of the Civil War.

Volunteers at Civil War field hospitals often wrote letters for wounded soldiers.

showed "all the qualities of American womanhood," he said. Now it was his turn "to be of service to the little nurse of Gettysburg."

Hundreds of brave women gave their time and risked their lives to serve the Union in the Civil War. They faced their difficulties with courage and made a difference.

WOMEN AND THE WAR

In the 1860s, women managed households, raised children, and helped their husbands. When the Civil War broke out, women lent their support.

The conflicts that led up to the war had been brewing for years. The states disagreed on several issues, but the root argument was slavery. Many Northerners

Slaves labored on large cotton plantations in the South in the 1800s.

7

opposed slavery and didn't want it to spread to new states. Abolitionists wanted to end it completely.

Slave owners in the South believed slaves were necessary. Vast fields of cotton and tobacco were among the crops that prospered in the long growing season. Small farmers and plantation owners depended on black slaves to do the backbreaking farmwork.

An 1860 presidential campaign banner for the Republican Party

8

Southerners didn't want Abraham Lincoln to be elected president in 1860. They believed he would put an end to slavery. Lincoln won the election, and seven Southern states seceded from the Union. Four more states would later follow their example.

In February 1861, seceding states formed a separate country called the Confederate States of America. They chose Jefferson Davis as their president. On April 12, 1861, Confederate troops attacked and took control of Fort Sumter in South Carolina.

The Union declared war

CHARLESTON

MERCURY

EXTRA:

Passed unanimously at 1.15 o'clock, P. M., December 20th, 1860.

AN ORDINANCE

To dissolve the Union between the State of South Carolina and other States united with her under the compact entitled " The Constitution of the United States of America."

We, the People of the State of South Carolina, in Convention assembled, do declare and ordain, and it is hereby declared and ordained,

That the Ordinance adopted by us in Convention, on the twenty-third day of May, in the year of our Lord one thousand seven hundred and eighty-eight, whereby the Constitution of the United States of America was ratified, and also, all Acts and parts of Acts of the General Assembly of this State, ratifying amendments of the said Constitution, are hereby repealed; and that the union now subsisting between South Carolina and other States, under the name of "The United States of America," is hereby dissolved.

THE

UNION

IS

DISSOLVED!

South Carolina's secession from the Union was announced in a newspaper on December 20, 1860.

9

on the Confederacy, vowing to bring back the states that had left. Lincoln said, "No state, upon its own mere notion, can lawfully get out of the Union."

Friends and relatives on opposite sides of the war began fighting one another. Men's lives changed as they marched off to battle. Women's lives also became very different.

Women workers filled bullets with ammunition at the U.S. Arsenal at Watertown, Massachusetts, during the Civil War.

Women had to manage the money, discipline the children, and run the farm or family business. Some Union women moved to cities and took jobs in factories, offices, schools, hospitals, and homes. The need for Army uniforms, bullets, and tents created hundreds of jobs. Many women became nurses and schoolteachers, jobs held mostly by men before the war.

Hundreds of courageous women took a more active role in the war. They headed to field hospitals, Army camps, and battlefields. They served as nurses, doctors, soldiers, and spies. Often they risked their lives to help the Union Army.

SUPPORT ON
THE HOME FRONT

At first, people thought the war would be short and easy. Patriotic Americans rallied to support it. Women encouraged their husbands, sons, and boyfriends to enlist. They sent men off to war in a flurry of parades. Some townspeople sponsored picnics and gave out sandwiches as

An enthusiastic crowd greeted the 6th Ohio Infantry as it passed through Cincinnati, Ohio, on May 17, 1861.

soldiers passed by on their way to battle.

As the fighting dragged on, people realized the war would be long. On the home front, women formed volunteer aid societies to collect and make items soldiers needed. The federal government was not supplying enough food, clothing, and arms for them. Hardworking women made quilts, knitted socks, and sewed uniforms. They rolled bandages and packed supplies.

When African-American men enlisted in the Army, black women formed their own soldiers' aid societies. Sojourner Truth, noted speaker, abolitionist, and former slave, was one of the women who helped organize supplies for Union soldiers.

Women also held fund-raisers to support the U.S. Sanitary Commission. This organization was in

Sojourner Truth (c. 1797–1883)

13

Workers gathered outside the U.S. Sanitary Commission in Washington, D.C.

charge of soldiers' medical care and supplies. Wealthy free black women raised large sums of money for organizations like the Colored Women's Sanitary Commission and hospitals for black soldiers.

Mary Abigail Dodge used her writing talent to compose magazine articles that convinced women to participate in the war effort. Newspaper writer Jane Grey Swisshelm wrote articles that inspired soldiers to fight and motivated people to help out however they could.

Anna Dickinson used her speaking ability to encourage women to support the war. Frances Ellen Watkins Harper, an African-American, gave speeches that brought attention to the abilities of black soldiers and urged people to donate money.

Musicians also backed the war effort. People sang at patriotic events, parades, and family gatherings. In 1861, poet Julia Ward Howe was inspired by a visit to a Union Army camp. She got up in the middle of the night and wrote the words to a rousing battle song. Sung to the tune of "John Brown's Body," the song became the popular "Battle Hymn of the Republic."

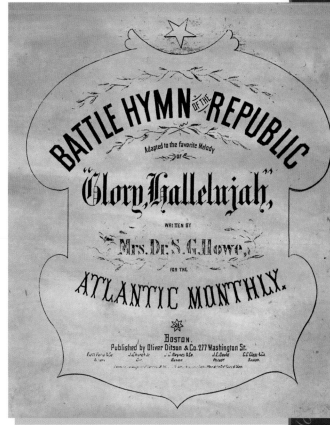

"Battle Hymn of the Republic" was published in Boston, Massachusetts, in 1862.

15

ANGELS OF MERCY

While many women supported the war from home, others took a more active role. Before the Civil War, nurses were primarily men. Now thousands of women became nurses and tended to sick and wounded soldiers. Hospitals were

*Nurse Mary Ann Bickerdyke offered a wounded soldier
a drink after a Civil War battle.*

set up in schools, town halls, old hotels, tents, and ships. Some nurses served at Army camps and on the battlefields. These women became known as angels of mercy.

Women became nurses for different reasons. Some believed God had called them to help relieve human suffering. Others thought a nurse was the next best thing to being a soldier. Famous writer Louisa May Alcott, author of *Little Women*, wrote in her diary why she became a nurse. "I've longed to be a man," she said, "but as I can't fight, I will content myself with working for those who can."

Most nurses had little or no formal training. Often they didn't know how to change a bandage. But they quickly learned to administer

Louisa May Alcott (1832–1888)

17

medicine and dress wounds.

Nurses worked day and night and often slept on cots in corners of the hospital. They cleaned, fed soldiers, ordered food and supplies, and wrote letters to soldiers' families. A hospital supervisor said, "There are so few of us that our nurses must do anything and everything—make beds, wait upon anybody, and often half a dozen at a time." Only nurses with nerves of steel helped during surgeries. They assisted doctors who operated on soldiers and performed amputations. Usually soldiers had nothing more than whiskey to ease their pain.

Nurses ate what soldiers ate—usually old, greasy bacon and thick, tough crackers called hardtack. Sometimes soldiers came close to starving. Nurse Clara Barton wrote in her diary, "I saw crowded into one old sunken hotel, lying helpless upon its bare, wet, bloody floors, five hundred fainting men hold up their cold, bloodless, dingy hands as I passed, and beg me in Heaven's name for a cracker to keep them from starving."

Nurses of the Michigan Soldiers' Relief Society tended to soldiers at a Union field hospital.

Germs and infections spread quickly among soldiers in hospitals. Nurses also got sick. Hundreds of ill, exhausted, homesick nurses returned to their homes. Then those who stayed had to work even harder.

FAMOUS WOMEN DOCTORS

There were not enough doctors to treat all the wounded, and female doctors were rare. In 1849, Dr. Elizabeth Blackwell became the first American woman to graduate from medical school. Later, her sister Emily also received a medical degree. During the Civil War, the Blackwell sisters organized the Women's Central Relief Association. They selected and trained nurses to serve in the war.

Dr. Elizabeth Blackwell (1821–1910)

Dr. Mary Edwards Walker tried to join the Union Army as a medical officer, but paid women doctors were not allowed. She volunteered her services and became the first female Army surgeon. She

20

treated Union soldiers but also went into Confederate territory to provide medical care for Southern citizens. Some believed she was acting as a spy. In 1864, she was captured by Confederate soldiers and imprisoned until she was rescued by Union soldiers four months later.

Dr. Mary Edwards Walker (1832–1919)

21

Surgeons and nurses at the U.S. Sanitary Commission tent at Gettysburg, Pennsylvania

Throughout the rest of the war, Walker assisted male surgeons at field hospitals near Union battlefields. After the war, in 1865, she was awarded the Congressional Medal of Honor for Meritorious Service for her contributions during the war.

COURAGEOUS NURSES

Although she had no formal nurse's training, Dorothea Dix was appointed superintendent of all female nurses in the Union Army. Dix had strict requirements for nurses. A woman had to have good character, plain looks, and be more than 30 years old. She couldn't wear colorful clothing, bows, curls, or jewelry. Dix recruited more than 2,000 nurses.

Dorothea Dix (1802–1887)

Clara Barton recognized early in the war that the Union Army was not prepared to care for all the wounded. In 1861 she set up her own agency to raise money and distribute supplies to soldiers. The government gave her permission to help the wounded soldiers of the Union as well as the Confederacy. She risked her life to help soldiers during several battles.

Barton said, "I did not wait for reporters and journalists to tell us that a battle had been fought. I went in while the battle raged." Sometimes Barton was so close to the action that the gunfire left blue powder on her face. The services Barton performed later became the foundation for the American Red Cross, which she founded in 1881.

In 1862, 30-year-old Louisa May Alcott arrived at Union Hospital near Washington, D.C.

Clara Barton (1821–1912)

YOUR RED CROSS NEEDS YOU!

The Red Cross, founded by Clara Barton after the Civil War, later recruited volunteers for World War II.

25

During its occupation, the Union Army built a hospital in Hilton Head, South Carolina.

Immediately, wounded soldiers started pouring in from the defeat at the Battle of Fredericksburg. Alcott and her supervisor, Hannah Ropes, saw how the wounded were suffering and treated poorly. They worked tirelessly to improve the quality of medical care. Ropes was a strong, determined nurse who went directly to the secretary of war with her complaints.

Alcott later wrote in her book, *Hospital Sketches*, "I often longed to groan for them, while the bed shook with the irrepressible [uncontrollable] tremor of their tortured bodies." Both women caught typhoid pneumonia in 1863, a disease they probably contracted from their patients.

Mary Ann Bickerdyke was in charge of field hospitals for Union General Ulysses S. Grant and General William T. Sherman. She was a tough-talking woman who stopped at nothing to feed and comfort her soldiers. She took supplies without permission and ignored doctors' orders so she could get her own job done.

A surgeon once asked Bickerdyke who gave her permission to do what she was doing. She replied, "On the authority of Lord God Almighty. Have you anything that outranks that?"

African-American Harriet Tubman was a dedicated field nurse for the Union. Massachusetts Governor John

Harriet Tubman (c. 1820–1913)

Susie King Taylor (1848–1912)

Andrew personally asked her to serve in military camps. Tubman moved from camp to camp throughout the war, cooking and using her special knowledge of roots and herbs to treat the injured.

Susie King Taylor, a former slave, accompanied her husband's all-black regiment. At first she cooked and did laundry. Then she taught soldiers how to read and write. When she saw the most seriously ill soldiers, she didn't hesitate to use her talents as a nurse.

In 1902 she published *Reminiscences of My Life in Camp* to prove that "there were

In 1864, a French newspaper depicted African-American women working at a Union Army camp.

'loyal women,' as well as men, in those days, who did not fear shell or shot, who cared for the sick and dying; women who camped and fared as the boys did."

Daughters of the Regiment and Vivandières

Women often stayed at Army camps for months or even years. Some were called Daughters of the Regiment. These young women were usually officers' relatives. They were

Women often visited or stayed at Union Army camps during the Civil War.

also called *vivandières*, a French word meaning women who supply food to soldiers.

Their roles depended on what needed to be done. Some rode a horse and carried a flag into battle. Others brought water and ammunition to soldiers on the battlefield. Vivandières dragged wounded men off the field and covered the faces of those who had died. Most vivandières carried the regiment's flag in parades and reviews.

These women donned uniforms. The jackets and pants resembled the soldiers' uniforms, but they added lace and a knee-length skirt to make them feminine.

Mary Tebe, who enlisted with her husband in 1861, carried the flag for the 27th Pennsylvania Volunteers in 13

Mary Tebe was a vivandière with two Pennsylvania infantry regiments.

31

battles and was wounded once. Soldiers called Anna Etheridge "Gentle Annie," but she was a strong vivandière and nurse. She helped wounded soldiers at many battles, including both battles at Bull Run and the Battle of Gettysburg.

Kady Brownell became a skilled sharpshooter and swordswoman during her stay at camp. Wearing her sword, she proudly carried the flag for her husband's Rhode Island regiment. In the chaos of one battle, she held the flag high while bullets screeched overhead. The scattered troops saw the flag in the midst of the thick smoke and rallied.

Kady Brownell in her vivandière uniform

SOLDIERS IN DISGUISE

Women were not allowed to fight. But several hundred women did not let that stop them. Disguised as men, they secretly joined the Union Army. Usually, they had no problem passing the medical exam required to enlist. Most examiners only made sure the men could march and shoot a gun.

Women often remained disguised as men for months or years. If discovered, a woman simply joined another regiment. It wasn't hard for a woman to maintain her disguise in the loose-fitting uniform that she rarely had to take off.

Jennie Hodgers served three years in the 95th Illinois Infantry. She fought as Albert Cashier throughout the war and maintained her male identity the rest of her life. When asked why she joined the Army, she replied, "The country needed men, and I wanted excitement."

Most women enlisted in the Army because they were patriotic. Some joined for money and others for adventure and independence. Many enlisted for love.

33

Frances Clayton wanted to be with her husband, so she enlisted in a Minnesota regiment in 1861. Disguised as a male soldier named Clalin, she served until December 1862, when she was injured and her husband was killed in battle. In a hospital with a bullet in her hip, Clayton's

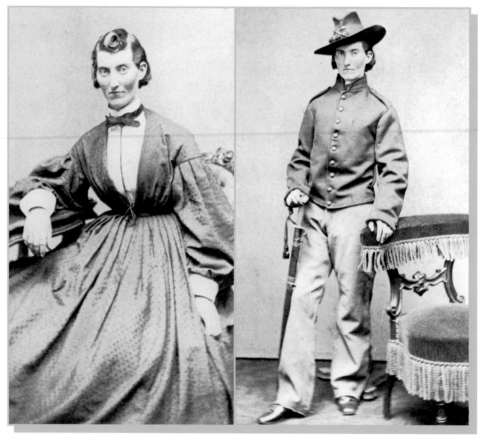

Frances Clayton disguised herself as a male soldier named Clalin.

Sarah Edmonds disguised herself as a male soldier named Franklin Thompson.

gender was discovered. She was discharged from the Army.

Nineteen-year-old Sarah Emma Edmonds joined a Michigan regiment and called herself Franklin Thompson. When asked why she became a soldier, she said, "I am naturally fond of adventure, a little ambitious, and a good deal romantic, but patriotism was the true secret of my success." Edmonds fought in several battles, including the first Battle of Bull Run and the Battle of Antietam. When she became ill with malaria, she was afraid workers at a military hospital might discover she was a woman. She went to a private hospital and never returned as a soldier.

35

Most of the Civil War battles were fought in the South.

There may have been hundreds more Northern women who fought as soldiers during the war. We may never know how many, because their true identities were not in the official records.

FAMOUS UNION SPIES

Hundreds of women served as spies for the Union during the Civil War. While some spied occasionally, others risked their lives on a regular basis. Actress Pauline Cushman wanted adventure, and she found it as a spy for the North.

Actress Pauline Cushman dressed up as a male soldier to spy on the Confederates.

37

Pretending to support the Confederacy, she gathered information and made lists of people who were anti-Union. Confederates eventually became suspicious of her. In 1863, she was arrested and sentenced to hang. Union troops helped her escape three days before her scheduled hanging, and she returned to her acting career. President Lincoln made her an honorary major in the Army.

One of the most daring and successful Union spies was Elizabeth Van Lew. Although she lived in the Confederate state of Virginia, Van Lew secretly supported the Union. Confederate leaders were often guests in her elegant home. She listened to what they said and passed on information to Union leaders. Members of her

38

Elizabeth Van Lew (1818–1900)

spy ring, many of them freed slaves, carried maps, documents, and messages in secret code to the North. They hid information in food baskets, hooped skirts, and secret compartments inside the soles of their shoes.

Mary Elizabeth Bowser, a free black woman, was part of Van Lew's group. She went undercover as a maid in the home of Confederate President Jefferson Davis. As she worked, she read documents and overheard Confederate plans. She passed on information almost daily to other spies who stopped by the president's home to make deliveries. When Confederates became

Mary Elizabeth Bowser secretly gathered information from Confederate President Jefferson Davis.

39

suspicious, Bowser fled to the North. Bowser's name was later placed in the U.S. Army's Military Intelligence Corps Hall of Fame.

Harriet Tubman, a runaway slave and abolitionist, spent many years working with the Underground Railroad. She helped thousands of slaves escape to free states and Canada on secret routes. Tubman also served as a Union scout and spy. Pretending to be an old woman, she moved easily through Confederate territory. In 1863, she led a raid in South Carolina that resulted in the escape of more than 700 slaves. Impressed by the success of this mission, a Union officer remarked, "This is the only military command in America wherein a woman, black or white, led the raid and under whose inspiration it was originated and conducted."

Women served the Union in many ways during the Civil War. Some worked hard behind the scenes to keep their families and businesses strong. Others played more active roles as factory workers, writers, speakers, nurses,

The brave women of the Union who served on battlefields and in hospitals and factories influenced the war and changed the role of women in the United States.

soldiers, and spies. But whether they served on the home front, in the workplace, or on the battlefield, these women of the Union made a difference in the Civil War and left their mark on history.

GLOSSARY

abolitionists—people who supported the banning of slavery

Confederacy—the Southern states that fought against the Northern states in the Civil War

enlist—to voluntarily join a branch of the military

field nurse—a nurse who serves on or near a battlefield

plantation—a large farm usually worked by slaves

pneumonia—an inflammation or infection of the lungs

regiment—a military group consisting of about 1,000 soldiers

secede—to withdraw from a group

Union—the Northern states that fought against the Southern states in the Civil War

vivandière—a woman who provided food and drink for Army soldiers

Did You Know?

- In medical school, Elizabeth Blackwell was not allowed to attend certain lectures about the human body because they were considered too embarrassing and not fit for a woman.

- Jane Newton Woolsey of New York and her six daughters collected and distributed supplies to Union hospitals from their home. Daughters Jane, Eliza, and Georgeanna became nurses. Georgeanna helped establish the Connecticut Training School for Nurses and wrote a nursing handbook.

- During the Civil War, chloroform was used to put a soldier to sleep during surgery. When it was not available, nurses gave the patient whiskey and a bullet to bite down on.

- Sarah Rosetta Wakeman, disguised as a Union soldier named Lyons Wakeman, died in 1864. Her identity remained a secret until her letters from the battlefront were published in the 1990s.

- In 1917, the Congressional Medal of Honor was taken away from Dr. Mary Edwards Walker. Congress changed the standards to include only actual combat with an enemy. Walker refused to give back her medal and wore it until her death in 1919. In 1977, the Army reinstated her medal.

IMPORTANT DATES

Timeline

1860	In November, Abraham Lincoln is elected president of the United States; in December, South Carolina secedes from the Union.
1861	In April, Confederate troops attack Fort Sumter, and the Civil War begins; Dorothea Dix is appointed superintendent of female nurses of the Union Army; the Women's Central Relief Association, led by Dr. Elizabeth Blackwell, is formed in New York City to recruit female nurses.
1862	Louisa May Alcott begins serving as a nurse at Union Hospital in Washington, D.C.
1863	Dr. Mary Edwards Walker volunteers to be a surgeon in the Union Army; Harriet Tubman becomes the first woman to lead Union troops on a military raid of Confederate property; actress Pauline Cushman, a spy for the Union, is captured by Confederate soldiers but later rescued by Union soldiers.
1865	The Civil War ends.

IMPORTANT PEOPLE

CLARA BARTON (1821–1912)

Civil War nurse who established her own agency to aid both Union and Confederate soldiers; she founded the American Red Cross in 1881

ELIZABETH BLACKWELL (1821–1910)

The first American woman to graduate from medical school; she organized the Women's Central Relief Association to select and train nurses to serve the Union in the Civil War

DOROTHEA DIX (1802–1887)

Medical reformer who served the Union as superintendent of nurses during the Civil War

HARRIET TUBMAN (1820–1913)

Runaway slave who served as a nurse, scout, and spy during the Civil War

MARY EDWARDS WALKER (1832–1919)

First woman to become a surgeon in the U.S. Army and to earn the Congressional Medal of Honor

WANT TO KNOW MORE?

At the Library

Alcott, Louisa May. *Hospital Sketches*. Boston: Bedford/St. Martin's, 2004.

Chang, Ina. *A Separate Battle: Women and the Civil War*. London: Puffin, 1996.

Currie, Stephen. *Women of the Civil War*. San Diego: Lucent Books, 2003.

Ford, Carin T. *Daring Women of the Civil War*. Berkeley Heights, N.J.: Enslow Publishers, 2004.

Furbee, Mary Rodd. *Outrageous Women of Civil War Times*. San Francisco: Jossey-Bass, 2003.

Schomp, Virginia. *The Civil War*. New York: Benchmark Books, 2004.

Silber, Nina. *Daughters of the Union: Northern Women Fight the Civil War*. Cambridge, Mass.: Harvard University Press, 2005.

On the Web

For more information on *Women of the Union*, use FactHound to track down Web sites related to this book.

1. Go to *www.facthound.com*

2. Type in this book ID: 0756520355

3. Click on the *Fetch It* button.

Your trusty FactHound will fetch the best Web sites for you!

On the Road

U.S. Army Women's Museum
2100 Adams Ave., Building P-5219
Fort Lee, VA 23801-2100
804/734-4326
Photographs, clothing, equipment, personal letters, and diaries of Army women past and present; Civil War battlefields and sites are nearby.

Gettysburg National Military Park and Museum
97 Taneytown Road
Gettysburg, PA 17325-2804
717/334-1124
Photographs and artifacts from the Gettysburg battlefield where Union and Confederate armies clashed

Look for more We the People books about this era:

The Assassination of Abraham Lincoln
ISBN 0-7565-0678-6

Battle of the Ironclads
ISBN 0-7565-1628-5

The Carpetbaggers
ISBN 0-7565-0834-7

The Confederate Soldier
ISBN 0-7565-2025-8

The Dred Scott Decision
ISBN 0-7565-2026-6

The Emancipation Proclamation
ISBN 0-7565-0209-8

Fort Sumter
ISBN 0-7565-1629-3

The Gettysburg Address
ISBN 0-7565-1271-9

Great Women of the Civil War
ISBN 0-7565-0839-8

The Lincoln-Douglas Debates
ISBN 0-7565-1632-3

The Missouri Compromise
ISBN 0-7565-1634-X

The Reconstruction Amendments
ISBN 0-7565-1636-6

Surrender at Appomattox
ISBN 0-7565-1626-9

The Underground Railroad
ISBN 0-7565-0102-4

The Union Soldier
ISBN 0-7565-2030-4

Women of the Confederacy
ISBN 0-7565-2033-9

A complete list of We the People titles is available on our Web site:
www.compasspointbooks.com

INDEX

27th Pennsylvania Volunteers, 31
95th Illinois Infantry, 33

abolitionists, 8, 13, 40
Alcott, Louisa May, 17, 24, 26, 27
American Red Cross, 24
Andrew, John, 27–28
angels of mercy, 17

Barton, Clara, 18, 23–24
"Battle Hymn of the Republic"
    (Julia Ward Howe), 15
Battle of Antietam, 35
Battle of Fredericksburg, 26
Battle of Gettysburg, 4, 32
Battles of Bull Run, 32, 35
Bickerdyke, Mary Ann, 27
Blackwell, Elizabeth, 20
Blackwell, Emily, 20
Bowser, Mary Elizabeth, 39–40
Brownell, Kady, 32
Bushman, Sadie, 4–6

Clayton, Frances, 34–35
Colored Women's Sanitary
    Commission, 14
Confederate States of America, 9,
    10, 21, 38, 39, 40
Congressional Medal of Honor, 22
Cushman, Pauline, 37–38

Daughters of the Regiment, 30

Davis, Jefferson, 9, 39
Dickinson, Anna, 15
disguises, 33, 34, 35
Dix, Dorothea, 23
doctors, 20–22
Dodge, Mary Abigail, 14

Edmonds, Sarah Emma, 35
Etheridge, Anna, 32

Fort Sumter, 9

Gettysburg, Pennsylvania, 4, 32
Grant, Ulysses S., 27

hardtack, 18
Harper, Frances Ellen Watkins, 15
Hodgers, Jennie, 33
Hospital Sketches (Louisa May
    Alcott), 27
hospitals, 4, 11, 14, 16–17, 18, 19, 22,
    24, 26–27
Howe, Julia Ward, 15

jobs, 11

Lincoln, Abraham, 9, 10, 38

magazine articles, 14–15
Military Intelligence Corps Hall of
    Fame, 40
musicians, 15

newspaper articles, 14–15

nurses, 11, 16, 17–19, 20, 23, 26–27,
    28, 32

parades, 12
picnics, 12–13
plantations, 8

Reminiscences of My Life in Camp
    (Susie King Taylor), 28–29
Ropes, Hannah, 26–27

Sherman, William T., 27
slavery, 7–8, 9
soldiers, 33–36
spies, 21, 37–40
Swisshelm, Jane Grey, 14

Taylor, Susie King, 28
Tebe, Mary, 31–32
Truth, Sojourner, 13
Tubman, Harriet, 27–28, 40
typhoid pneumonia, 27

U.S. Sanitary Commission, 13–14
Underground Railroad, 40

Van Lew, Elizabeth, 38–39
vivandières, 31, 32
volunteer aid societies, 13

Walker, Mary Edwards, 20–22
Women's Central Relief
    Association, 20

About the Author

Alice Flanagan has written more than 100 titles for children and teachers. Her books include holidays, phonics for beginning readers, career guidance, biographies of U.S. presidents and first ladies, and informational books about famous people and events in American history. She lives with her husband in Chicago, Illinois. As a writer/photographer team, they have published several books together. Their travels have taken them to many places and brought them lifelong friends.